Steve Austin
THE STONE COLD STORY

Steve Austin
THE STONE COLD™ STORY

by Terry West

SCHOLASTIC INC.

New York   Toronto   London   Auckland   Sydney   Mexico City   New Delhi   Hong Kong

No part of this publication may be reproduced in whole or in part, or stored in a retrieval system, or transmitted in any form or by any means, electronic, mechanical, photocopying, recording, or otherwise, without written permission of the publisher. For information regarding permission, write to Scholastic Inc., Attention: Permissions Department, 555 Broadway, New York, NY 10012.

ISBN 0-439-24386-6

Copyright © 2001 Scholastic Inc. All rights reserved. Published by Scholastic Inc. SCHOLASTIC and associated logos are trademarks and/or registered trademarks of Scholastic Inc.

Designed by Peter Koblish

12   11   10   9   8   7   6   5   4   3   2   1   1   2   3   4   5/0

Printed in the U.S.A.
First Scholastic printing, January 2001

TABLE OF CONTENTS

Steve Austin

THE STONE COLD™ STORY

INTRODUCTION
The Strange World of Professional Wrestling

In the early 1900s, there was a huge audience for professional wrestling. Matches between opponents lasted for hours. Sometimes an audience would watch a single match involving two men for three or four hours!

But over time, people began to shy away from matches, citing that wrestling was often tedious and . . . well . . . boring.

As professional wrestling matured, a decision was made. Matches had to be shorter. But the only way to accomplish this was to orchestrate the matches. The outcome of a match was decided before the two wrestlers even entered the ring. Time limits were placed on matches to keep fans from leaving their seats. Wrestlers developed larger-than-life personalities to appeal to the audience.

Bad guys — or heels — were created for the audience to boo. Good guys — or babyfaces — were created for the audience to cheer. Heels were supposed to be cowards who would take advantage of an opponent whenever the opportunity arose. Babyfaces could take the punishment (which would put many of us in the hospital) and find the strength from the audiences' encouragement to rise up off the mat and pin their foes.

Over the years, wrestling reflected what was going on in the world. If the United States was at war with another nation, a villain supposedly from that country would soon emerge from the ranks of professional wrestling, eager to challenge the American hero of the day.

In the early 1980s, professional wrestling began to attract more and more fans, spurred by World Wrestling Federation (WWF) owner, Vince McMahon, Jr. Heroes such as Hulk Hogan and Jimmy "Superfly" Snuka fought notorious bad guys and used their flamboyant personas to make millions of dollars in merchandise.

Professional wrestling was enjoying its greatest success yet.

In the span of ten years, however, professional wrestling would change dramatically. Wrestlers filled with attitude began to challenge the concept of good guys and bad guys. And one wrestler in particular would forever blur the line between babyface and heel.

Stone Cold™ Steve Austin. With his penetrating blue eyes and swagger in the ring, Austin would take the sports entertainment field of wrestling and turn it upside down. This book is about the man behind the personality. The man actually named Steve Williams.

CHAPTER 1
Steven Williams

Steve Williams, the man who would one day shake the world of professional wrestling to its core, was born on December 18, 1964, in Victoria, Texas. However, he would not be there long enough to build childhood memories. His family moved to Edna, Texas, while Steve was still a baby.

Steve was a friendly child with blond hair and a soft smile. By fifth grade, he began watching professional wrestling on television. His love of the sport was deep and immediate. His parents tried to get him to go outside and play instead of watching television, but they couldn't pry him away from wrestling.

As a child, Steve was a far cry from the man we

know today as Stone Cold Steve Austin. Steve was kind of shy and always polite.

But by the time he attended Edna High School, he was so popular that his classmates voted him Class Favorite three years running. He also made the Honor Society.

It was during his high school years that Steve began to demonstrate his sense of humor. He was considered a class clown by many of the students and teachers. Believe it or not, this trait would one day prove invaluable to Steve as a professional wrestler. Steve could entertain, which is one of the most valuable qualities a professional wrestler can possess.

The other necessary attribute of a professional wrestler is athletic ability. And Steve had a truckload of that. In high school, he joined the track and field team; his event was throwing the discus. He also played football.

Steve's performance on the football field earned him a scholarship to the North Texas State University in Denton, Texas (now known as the University of North Texas). Steve attended classes and played for the Denton Eagles for most of 1985 and 1986. He started out as a linebacker, but as his football abilities grew, Steve shifted to defensive tackle.

While pursuing a degree in physical education, Steve battled his bad knees, but he finished every game of his senior year. And though he was considered a fantastic football player (coach Corky Nelson once commented that Steve was born to play football), Steve felt that he wasn't good enough to play professionally.

So, after the season was over, Steve made a tough choice. He left North Texas State University without a degree. His scholarship money was gone, and he didn't think college was the route for him, either. Steve paid for one semester out of his own pocket, but it was too difficult to work to pay for his schooling and go to classes full time. So, he took a job unloading trucks on a freight dock.

However, this wasn't quite what he had planned for his future, either.

Young, frustrated, and still not sure where his destiny would lead him, Steve made the best of his job. He *had* to make a living. But if he was going to be a dockworker, then he would be the best dockworker that he could be. This determination is another trait that would help Steve find success one day.

When many would grumble and complain at the hard work and only do what was required of them and no more, Steve threw himself into the job. He paid his bills and tried to make the best of the situation.

It wasn't too long after this, however, that the square ring would come calling . . .

THE BOTTOM LINE: Steve Austin had to change his name early in his career because another wrestler, Steve "Dr. Death" Williams, was already using it.

CHAPTER 2
Wrestling with the Future

It was during the long and tiring hours of his dockworker's job that Steve saw a television commercial for the Chris Adams wrestling school. The advertisement promised to take young men who had determination and skill and turn them into professional wrestlers.

Steve's mind was instantly transported back to his childhood days, watching wrestling on TV while his parents tried to get him to go outside and play. Steve had also spent much of his free time watching wrestlers at the Sportatorium arena in Dallas, Texas. He figured he could become as good in the ring as the wrestlers he had watched in those days. Wrestlers such as the VonErich brothers and the Fabulous Freebirds. Iceman King Parsons and Bruiser Brody.

Even Gentleman Chris Adams, the British-born baby-face who was running the wrestling school. If they could make a name for themselves, so could he.

In 1989, Steve entered the school with determination and confidence. But he soon realized that he didn't really know anything about professional wrestling. His first lesson was the most important of all: learning how to take a bump without breaking his neck.

"Taking a bump" is a wrestling term that means knowing how to fall and land on the hard, unforgiving ring mat without causing yourself injury. In the heat of a match, taking a bad fall can spell disaster for a professional wrestler. Knowing which part of your body is best suited to absorb the impact of a bodyslam or a clothesline can mean a much longer career for a wrestler. He also learned basic wrestling moves, and how not to hurt another wrestler while performing those moves.

Steve graduated from the school in 1989. But even though he had a wrestling education, he also realized that, in a sense, there was no real formal education for professional wrestling. There are several aspects of the sport that you must learn by trial and error. The most important aspect, of course, is creating an interesting persona. Around this time,

Steve also began dating Jeanie Clark, Chris Adams's ex-wife, who would eventually marry Steve, and be with him on his way to the WCW.

In his first professional match at the Sportatorium, Steve beat wrestler Frogman Lablanc. In this first match, Steve looked nothing like the Stone Cold we know now. He had long blond hair. He was cocky, arrogant, flashy, and had more of a pretty-boy persona.

But Steve was talented and aggressive, two virtues that would serve him well. Later in 1989, he packed up and moved to Memphis, Tennessee, to work for the United States Wrestling Association (USWA). The USWA was a regional wrestling promotion association in Memphis that had its glory days in the mid-1980s. The feud between comedian Andy Kaufman and Jerry "The King" Lawler put the USWA on the map during those years.

Steve, still confident after his first professional win, would learn a few things from the USWA. He would learn that the road to stardom was long and stretched out well into the future.

And he wouldn't enjoy that stardom as a wrestler named Steve Williams.

THE BOTTOM LINE: Steve is an avid archer.

CHAPTER 3
Steve Austin Is Born

When Steve first arrived in Memphis, he was scheduled for a match the very next day. He had to fight wrestlers he had never worked with, and hope he could improvise his way through the matches. Like the matches in the World Wrestling Federation (WWF) and the World Championship Wrestling WCW, all the USWA matches were staged, but they still required some detailed choreography.

After his first match, the USWA told him he still had a lot to learn. They felt Steve had no charisma or honed in-ring ability. They made him watch matches while he continued to train.

The USWA saw that Steve had potential, and in a very short time, he would change their first evaluation of his abilities. His in-ring skills improved, but

Steve still needed to learn how to ratchet his personality up a few notches and bring the audience into his corner.

A major blow came when one of the promoters informed him that he would have to change his name. Another wrestler known as Steve "Dr. Death" Williams was working the same territory, so Steve would have to pick a different name to use as a professional wrestler. Now, put yourself in Steve's place. Imagine for one second that you were told to change your name just because someone else had that name, too. He wanted the world to know him as Steve Williams. It *was* his name, after all.

How Steve settled on Steve Austin has never been clear. One report states that a promoter had a television on that was showing a rerun of *The Six Million Dollar Man* (the main character was named Steve Austin) when Steve was told to change his name.

However it happened, Steve was reintroduced to the wrestling fans as Steve Austin. And soon he was learning yet another valuable lesson of the wrestling world: paying dues. In 1990, Steve was constantly on the road performing in house shows. (A house show is a non-televised event held at arenas in different cities.) He made very little money, and sometimes the only thing he could afford to eat was potatoes. He started to get discouraged and considered finding a new job.

But then Steve started a feud that helped make him more popular. He even earned the 1990 Rookie of the Year Award from the readers of *Pro Wrestling Illustrated.*

Now, to truly understand pro wrestling, you have to know that it is actually one giant soap opera with bodyslams. Chris Adams, Steve's teacher, started a feud with Steve about his ex-wife, Jeanie Clark (who would eventually marry Steve). In wrestling, storylines are often based on some aspect of reality. Chris Adams was Steve's mentor, and Steve was now seen in the company of Chris's ex-wife. It was very dramatic. Eventually, Adams versus Austin became the hottest feud in the USWA. While there is no actual proof that there were any bad feelings between Adams and Austin, professional wrestling does have a way of building up these feuds that are loosely based on a real situation.

Steve was finally beginning to build some steam.

In 1991, Steve was approached by WCW, which was owned by Ted Turner. It was a big move for

Steve. Operating out of Georgia, the WCW was one the biggest wrestling federations, second only to the WWF. It would be a huge boost for his career.

Steve accepted the offer, but soon found the WCW had another shocker for him: They didn't want Steve as a babyface wrestler. They wanted him to turn heel.

Turning heel was a hard decision for Steve. Babyface heroes like Hulk Hogan were making a ton of money off merchandising — selling T-shirts, posters, and other products to fans. The more popular a babyface wrestler was, the more merchandise that wrestler could sell. Hulk Hogan sold more merchandise in his heyday than any other pro wrestler. Becoming a heel could be very limiting for Steve. Besides, he had all the classic earmarks of a babyface: good looks, nice build, and baby blue eyes.

But it was a shot at the big time. Steve Austin knew that it was his big break.

THE BOTTOM LINE: Steve Austin's ex-wife, Jeanie Clark, became his valet in the WCW. She was known as Lady Blossom.

CHAPTER 4
Stunning Steve Austin

On May 31, 1991, Steve Austin debuted in the WCW. He defeated wrestler Sam Houston on a card in Houston, Texas. (A card is a line-up of matches for any given wrestling event.)

Steve was now in the big league. Before he'd been living hand to mouth, sometimes only getting paid twenty dollars for a night's work. Now he was making a good salary. It was a steady income.

Steve was introduced to the WCW fans as Stunning Steve Austin, a pretty boy wrestler with attitude. But he didn't "go over" right away with the fans. "Going over" is a wrestling term that means getting a good reaction from the crowd. He didn't get much heat, either. "Heat" is another wrestling term that means getting a bad response from the crowd. Heat is usually reserved for heels.

Steve wasn't sure how comfortable he was with his "Stunning" ring persona. The powers that be at WCW felt that he needed a gimmick. He just wasn't flashy enough, and his microphone skills needed work.

Steve wasn't happy about the WCW's attitude. He had grown up watching wrestlers who were no talk and all action. He wanted to be known as a fearsome brawler.

Plus, his pretty boy image was not going over that well with the audience. He needed to find another personality that would help him go over better. The WCW prodded him to come up with a new gimmick.

He was told that a guy in black tights with no charisma would never go over. Steve continued to fight this idea. What was wrong with a no-nonsense wrestler? One who came to the ring just to fight.

Despite these problems, Steve got a decent push from WCW management. He held the WCW Television Title for a while, until he lost it on April 27, 1992. On October 27, 1992, however, during a grueling match with Dusty Rhodes for the WCW Halloween Havoc pay-per-view, Steve finally got some recognition.

Dusty Rhodes was a huge wrestler known in his heyday as The American Dream. Rhodes was a tough-as-nails Texas wrestler who was famous for using his fists, but very few actual wrestling moves. The match ended in a draw, but Steve won something more important from that fateful match — fan recognition. The WCW management and fans began to notice him. He was viewed as an up-and-coming star.

The WCW were still in a quandary as to where Austin fit in to the scheme of the organization, but they gave him a decent raise and tried to help Steve figure out his future.

THE BOTTOM LINE: Steve designs most of his WWF merchandise.

CHAPTER 5
The Hollywood Blonds

During 1993, Steve teamed up with a wrestler known as Flyin' Brian Pillman. Pillman was a raspy-voiced, former professional linebacker for the Cincinnati Bengals football team. He had a mane of long, curly blond hair. At six feet tall and two-hundred-twenty-plus pounds, Brian was considered slight for a professional wrestler. But he had the heart of a champion and had fought adversity his whole life.

Pillman was diagnosed with throat cancer at a very young age. His raspy voice was a result of the numerous operations to cure that ailment. Pillman would fight pain throughout his entire wrestling career. He broke his ankle early in 1997 in a car accident (right before he was to enter the WWF). That ankle was fused together, causing him constant pain in the ring.

Austin and Pillman were portrayed as young lions, coming in to dethrone the older, more established grapplers of the WCW. They were cocky, arrogant, and challenged the old guard of the WCW. They were perceived as the next generation of WCW superstars.

The Hollywood Blonds, as they were known, were one of the most successful WCW tag teams of the 1990s (and, some argue, one of the best in WCW history). Unfortunately, backstage politics and personality clashes between The Hollywood Blonds and more established wrestlers would take its toll.

The Hollywood Blonds were getting heat, and the crowds were into their matches. They first won the coveted WCW tag team titles on March 2, 1993. The tag team titles are held by two wrestlers who work together in a match against two other wrestlers.

But this is where the problems started. The WCW has often been criticized for backstage politics. Some of the older wrestlers felt threatened by the rising popularity of The Hollywood Blonds. Bruised egos eventually led to the breakup of the popular tag team. And to add insult to injury, the WCW created a feud between Austin and Pillman.

Now, here were two guys who were the best of friends. Austin often spoke of the admiration he felt toward Brian Pillman, who Steve considered the smartest guy in wrestling. Brian's injury and his patience in dealing with it also taught Steve a lesson about wrestling against all odds. Although Steve has cited respect for many wrestlers, Brian Pillman has always been at the top of his list.

It made no sense — to the fans or Steve and Brian — that the Hollywood Blonds could be disbanded. But the egos of certain wrestlers, who remain unnamed to this day saw to it that the team was split before any more heat catapulted the duo to the top of the federation.

The policy of the WCW has always been to hold the younger talent back, allowing the more established superstars to bask in the limelight. Steve did not understand this philosophy. He and Brian had genuine heat, and were being punished for their popularity.

At the same time, Steve didn't feel that his mark in professional wrestling would be made as one of The Hollywood Blonds. Steve knew that he would walk the path to glory alone one day. In many ways, the pairing stifled his creativity. One of the reasons was that The Hollywood Blonds were a couple of obnoxious punks. He wanted the association between The Hollywood Blonds to last longer than it did, but he didn't want the partnership to last forever.

As mentioned before, some reality spills into the storylines that are created for the wrestling ring. Austin and Pillman made snide comments against the older WCW wrestlers during interview segments. That was part of their gimmick. But some honesty also slipped out between the rehearsed words Steve and Brian recited, too. Some of the longer-established WCW superstars were offended by their comments, and used them against the duo.

On August 18, 1993, The Hollywood Blonds lost the tag team titles to Ric Flair and Arn Anderson, two wrestlers who were on the far side of their prime. That was the punishment for The Hollywood Blonds.

THE BOTTOM LINE: Steve got inspiration for the name "Stone Cold" from his ex-wife, Jeanie Clark.

CHAPTER 6
The WCW U.S. Heavyweight Champion

After the end of The Hollywood Blonds, Steve joined a wrestling stable. (A stable is a group of wrestlers that form into one team and work under the guidance of a manager. It is a common practice for a federation to put several wrestlers together who are not getting enough individual heat from the audience.) Steve joined the Dangerous Alliance, managed by Paul E. Dangerously (Paul Heyman, who would eventually leave WCW and begin his own wrestling promotion, Extreme Championship Wrestling — the ECW).

After his tenure with the Dangerous Alliance, Steve was managed by Colonel Rob Barker. On December 27, 1993, Steve defeated longtime foe Dusty Rhodes and became the WCW U.S. Heavyweight Champion. The U.S. title is second only to the WCW World Heavyweight Championship Belt.

Steve managed to hold onto his title until August 24, 1994, when he lost it to a wrestler named Ricky Steamboat. Austin and Steamboat had feuded early in Austin's career over the television title.

Less than a month later, during a WCW house show, Steve injured his knee during a tough match against fan favorite Jim Duggan, who was a former football player with few wrestling skills. When you face Duggan, you face a brawler who will come at you with fists, clotheslines, and a two-by-four, if the referee isn't looking! It's no wonder Steve walked away from that match with an injury.

Steve used the time off to consider his options. He felt his talents were being wasted in the WCW. He knew he would only achieve mid-level success in that organization. It seemed that the prestigious WCW World Heavyweight Title would never come his way. And that had a lot to do with his motivation. Sure, the money is good. But, deep down, every wrestler wants to be at the top of the game. Every one of them wants to hold the world title — or at least be a top contender for it.

And Steve hadn't become a wrestler just for the money. Who would risk their health for 20 dollars a night unless the desire went deeper than cash in their pockets? There were much easier ways to make money. Steve also wanted the respect and attention he felt he deserved.

But Eric Bischoff, the head of WCW, talked Steve out of quitting the organization. Bischoff told Austin he was due for a major push (a "push" is when a wrestler is given the opportunity to further his career). Steve reluctantly agreed.

Steve was sent to Asia for a month to wrestle under the New Japan Pro Wrestling Federation. It is not uncommon for big U.S. wrestling federations like WCW to send their talent overseas to build a name for their organization. During a match, Steve tore a tricep muscle. It was a tough injury. But to his credit, Steve finished the tour of Japan. He must have used the same determination and willpower his close friend Brian Pillman taught him.

Steve returned to the States, and immediately underwent surgery and rehab to fix the torn muscle. He would be out of ring action for months.

THE BOTTOM LINE: Steve loves his home state of Texas so much that he has it tattooed on his calf.

CHAPTER 7
Don't Trust Anybody

Now, if you're a fan of Steve Austin, then you notice that he has a lot of anger toward authority. His attacks on WWF owner Vince McMahon are legendary.

Again, let's talk about truth that seeps into the made-up wrestling stories. . . .

It was 1994. Steve had enjoyed minor success in the WCW as a three-time champion: He had held the television, U.S., and tag team belts at various times.

Steve felt that most of his hassles about "going over" had to do with backstage politics. Let's also not forget that by this time, WWF mainstay Hulk Hogan had defected to the WCW. The WCW was in a transition period. It was trying to compete with the more popular WWF. When they brought Hogan and other familiar WWF wrestlers to their camp, the WCW started slowly phasing out their existing talent. They had to. Hulk Hogan got a huge paycheck, which meant that some of the WCW's overhead had to be cut.

Steve had worked hard for the WCW. He had performed like a consummate professional. He had given his best, as he had on his high school and college football teams, as he had in the USWA, when he could barely afford to eat . . . even as hard as he had worked unloading trucks on a dock. He had gone along with anything the WCW had thrown at him (including another grudge match with mentor Chris Adams — an attempt to cash in on the USWA feud that had brought Steve so much attention).

At this point, Steve was prepared to leave the WCW. He could see the writing on the wall. The invasion of WWF wrestlers meant that existing talent would be pushed aside. Steve didn't want to get lost in the shuffle. He'd had his ups and downs, during his years of employment in the WCW but he felt he had only scratched the surface of his career. Eric Bischoff had talked him out of leaving the WCW, however.

But while he was recuperating from the tricep injury, Steve received a phone call at his home in Atlanta, Georgia (where he had moved to be closer to the WCW). He was fired over the telephone by Eric Bischoff! Steve's contract had a 90-day clause. If Steve was unable to wrestle for 90 days or longer, he could be fired.

Steve was outraged. What bothered him the most, though, was being fired over the phone. He felt the least the WCW could have done was fire him face to face.

Steve was now back to square one. He had an injury that would take time to heal. And now he had a wife and children to support.

Steve took the only option he felt was available to him at the time. He contacted Paul Heyman, his former manager in the Dangerous Alliance and owner of the ECW.

THE BOTTOM LINE: Steve loves driving big vehicles! In the WWF, he has driven to the ring in a pickup truck, monster truck, an 18-wheeler, and a zamboni (a vehicle used to clean ice rinks).

CHAPTER 8
Extreme Superstar

Extreme Championship Wrestling built a name for itself on brutal, bloody matches. Operating out of Philadelphia, the ECW gained a cult following that made them into the third most-known federation and has gained recognition for many of their wrestlers. ECW superstars such as The Dudley Boyz, Taz, Raven, and others have gone on to greater glory in the WCW and WWF.

Steve's move to the ECW was a brief, but extremely important stepping-stone in his career. Billed as the Extreme Superstar, Austin debuted in ECW at their September 16, 1995, pay-per-view, "Gangstas Paradise."

Steve, who was still recovering from his injury, did many shoot interviews during which he vented his anger and frustration at the WCW. (A shoot interview is an interview in which a wrestler is allowed to improvise his lines and speak honestly without management's approval.) In these interviews, the Stone Cold™ attitude was starting to emerge.

It was easy for Steve to do. He was telling the truth. The WCW had treated him badly, and he retaliated with his microphone skills . . . skills he was given very little opportunity to hone with the WCW. He talked about the WCW politics and how he had been held back from greatness. He even dressed up and made fun of Hulk Hogan, a wrestler he felt was past his prime, and who was responsible for much of the backstage power plays going on in the WCW. He also put the ECW down on many occasions. He blasted the ECW for their more violent storylines. He was a wrestler. He had come to Philadelphia to wrestle.

Unfortunately, because of his injury Steve only wrestled three matches in the ECW. But he gained more than he could ever realize from his days in "barbwire city" (a nickname given the ECW by other wrestlers because of its more violent storylines).

Steve learned to work the crowd. He could make

the audience angry at him. The ECW fans perceived Steve as a wrestler from a bigger federation, who waltzed into the ECW arena and insulted the wrestlers, organization, and fans. The ECW wasn't good enough for him, he would say.

Steve still didn't have a gimmick. He was himself . . . a disgruntled man who had given the best of himself to a company that had stabbed him in the back for his hard work and dedication. He told it like it was.

His microphone skills were improving with every ECW segment. But, again, Steve felt his future with the ECW was in doubt. He was not granted any title matches. Management may have felt that granting Steve a world title reign might have undermined the ECW's existing talent. By letting Steve win the title, they would have admitted that Steve was right — that a wrestler from a bigger federation could come in and totally dominate the ECW ranks. It would not have been a good business move.

Steve might have damaged his own potential career in the ECW with his shoot interviews. But at least he had managed to hone his ability to work the crowd.

After a few months, Steve decided he had gotten all he could from the ECW. Once again, he was trying to put his hands on that destiny that had eluded him since 1989. But by the end of 1995, there was a light at the end of the tunnel.

And it was coming from the raging locomotive commonly known as the WWF.

THE BOTTOM LINE: The Million Dollar Belt, a title handed to Steve by Ted DiBiase in Steve's early WWF days, is not a sanctioned title. It is the property of DiBiase, who had worn it in the past as the self-professed Million Dollar Champion.

CHAPTER 9
The Ringmaster

On the December 18, 1995, episode of the USA Network's WWF program, *Monday Night Raw,* Steve Austin debuted as The Ringmaster™.

The Ringmaster was managed by Ted DiBiase, a former top heel who became famous as the WWF villain The Million Dollar Man™. The Ringmaster was DiBiase's Million Dollar Champion. For the role, Steve wore a belt that looked like it was studded with diamonds.

Saying Steve did not like the character of The Ringmaster would be a huge understatement. But he had finally managed to work his way back into a major federation, and he was willing to work the kinks out of the character as time passed. Working for the WWF was an opportunity that Steve would give anything for. Desperate for talent as the WCW began to beat them in popularity (by now, ex-WWF superstars Scott Hall and Kevin Nash were appearing on weekly WCW television programs), the WWF was working closely with young talent, hoping to find the next Hulk Hogan or The Ultimate Warrior to put them back at the top of the sports entertainment world.

Steve knew his destiny in the WWF was to wear the World Championship belt. But he also knew there was a pecking order and that dues had to be paid before that could happen.

His destiny would never be fulfilled by The Ringmaster. He felt that he was more of a sidekick to DiBiase than an actual wrestler. Steve soon found himself at his wit's end again. He needed a gimmick, but despised the idea of a glitzy pretty boy.

His blond locks were shed first on his search for a new persona. He got a crew cut, and the babyface and friendly blue eyes of Steve Austin began to take on a new look. The anger and frustration he had lived with for the last few years began to show, etched angrily on his face.

Steve finally shaved his head completely, giving

The Ringmaster a more threatening look. He topped off this metamorphosis with a neatly trimmed goatee.

It didn't help the character. The Ringmaster was engaged in a floundering feud with another WWF superstar, Savio Vega. At the climax of this under-card feud, Ted DiBiase left the WWF for the greener pastures of the WCW, leaving The Ringmaster on his own. Steve had to do something fast — before his career in the WWF was completely jeopardized by The Ringmaster gimmick.

This is the kind of situation in which the WCW and WWF differ dramatically. In the WCW, Steve had been told to just follow the guidance of the bookers (the men who book matches and have a lot of say in the wrestlers' personalities), and to do what was best for the company. And, when being a company guy didn't get him the attention he worked so hard for, he was fired. In the WWF, wrestlers are encouraged to better themselves, to come up with interesting ideas and character developments. A wrestler that begins to garner attention is not held back. In the WWF, the audience decides the future of a wrestler. Cheer a wrestler on, and WWF owner Vince McMahon listens. At this point in his WWF career, those cheers were still in the future for Steve Austin. But he was given the opportunity to work for them.

And soon he would stumble onto his new wrestling personality, quite by accident . . .

THE BOTTOM LINE: One wrestler Steve Austin admires greatly is his former WCW tag team partner, Brian Pillman, who died from a heart attack in 1997. Every year, a Brian Pillman Memorial Wrestling card is organized to raise money for Brian's wife and children.

CHAPTER 10
Stone Cold Steve Austin

It is the stuff of which legends are made.

While trying to capture a new image, Steve had already shaved his head. This was not a tremendous sacrifice. He had a receding hairline, and was beginning to go bald.

Steve was starting to cultivate the new look, but needed a new persona to be add to this image. The WWF tried to help by providing him with lists of personalities and names that would reshape the faltering Ringmaster into a strong WWF force.

But none of them sat well with Austin.

He knew what he was going for . . . a brutal grappler, filled with rage and frustration, who came to the ring because he enjoyed beating people up.

But the name still eluded him. Audiences weren't responding to The Ringmaster, whether he had bright blond hair or a cleanly shaved head.

One morning, Steve was agonizing over the fact that he couldn't come up with a name for his new character. His wife, Jeanie, brought him a cup of hot tea. She told him to drink his tea before it turned stone cold . . .

It was that simple.

Over a cup of morning tea, Steve Austin had a new identity. Stone Cold Steve Austin was born.

Steve met with Vince McMahon, the WWF owner, to discuss his new ring persona. McMahon listened to Steve, and liked what he heard. McMahon is known for listening to his employees, and trying to help them be as successful as possible. While the WWF turned wrestlers into superstars, the WCW was, at this point in time, raiding the ranks of the WWF. Seeking to build the new WCW on proven talent and using owner Ted Turner's money, the WCW had lured several big names from the WWF.

While Vince McMahon is certainly successful and wealthy, he could not compete with Ted Turner in a bidding war. At this time, the WCW was beating the WWF in a ratings war that pitted the two companies'

Monday night prime-time shows — WCW's *Monday Nitro* and WWF's *Monday Night Raw* — against each other.

Vince knew that the only way to turn his company around was to build new wrestling legends for the 1990s. Wrestling needed attitude injected into it.

Stone Cold Steve Austin would turn out to be Vince's spearhead in this revolution (but neither McMahon or Austin knew it at the time).

As soon as the character of Stone Cold Steve Austin was decided, Vince came up with the perfect venue to unleash this new force on the wrestling world.

The 1996 King of the Ring pay-per-view tournament.

THE BOTTOM LINE: Many WWF personalities have nicknamed Stone Cold the Texas Rattlesnake because he will attack anyone foolish enough to get in his way in the ring.

CHAPTER 11
The King of the Ring

Everyone has a defining moment.

Steve Austin's came the night of June 23, 1996, in the Mecca Arena in Milwaukee. It was the King of the Ring tournament.

In the King of the Ring tournament, 16 wrestlers fight in one-on-one battles. Losers are eliminated until only two combatants remain to face each other in a final match. The winner of that last match is declared the King of the Ring.

The WWF allows many up-and-coming superstars to win this match. It is usually the sign of a wrestler about to move up the ladder of success. In the past, wrestlers such as Shawn Michaels, Bret "The Hitman" Hart, and even Triple H™ have all won this significant tournament.

For this important night, Steve Austin had improved and made even more changes on the Stone Cold persona. His finishing move as The Ringmaster was a sleeper hold. A sleeper move is applied to the opponent's head. It cuts off the blood to the opponent's brain, causing him to pass out.

It had also been his former sponsor, Ted DiBiase's, finishing move. Steve knew this sleeper hold, dubbed "The Million Dollar Dream," would have to be eliminated from his arsenal. He needed a lethal move to complement his new persona — one that could be executed quickly and would get a big response from the crowd. He came up with a finishing move called the Stone Cold Stunner (perhaps in homage to his days as Stunning Steve Austin).

The Stunner is a move in which Steve turns his back to his opponent, wraps his arm around his opponent's head, positions his opponent's chin on his own shoulder, and then drops to the mat. The opponent falls to his knees, taking the impact of the fall right on the chin.

Though the move has been executed flawlessly hundreds of times by Austin, and no harm has ever been reported from applying the move, it still looks devastatingly painful.

In the second to last King of the Ring match,

Steve faced Marvelous Marc Mero, and dominated the entire match.

When all was said and done, Steve had won the match, but he still had to go backstage and have 18 stitches sewn into his lower lip. Marc had accidentally kicked Steve in the mouth, causing the wound.

But those stitches or the pain didn't stop Steve from meeting Jake "The Snake" Roberts in the final match. Roberts had earned the nickname The Snake because of his penchant for bringing a large snake to the ring, and was once considered the most fearsome wrestler in the business. He was cruel, calculating . . . and at times, pure evil.

Jake Roberts is a wrestler who Steve Austin has a lot of respect for. However, the Jake Roberts Steve faced that night was a shell of his former self. Jake had grown older, and was way past his prime in the ring.

Steve won the King of the Ring final match with relative ease. As Jake Roberts was helped out of the ring, Steve stepped up to his throne and participated in an interview segment.

It was during this segment that he would utter a motto that would cause a whirlwind of controversy and sell more wrestling merchandise than has ever been sold before . . .

THE BOTTOM LINE: Goldberg, a WCW wrestler fashioned after Stone Cold, once challenged Steve Austin on *The Tonight Show with Jay Leno.* Steve responded by saying that he would be happy to fight Goldberg, if Goldberg ever made it to the big league (meaning the WWF).

CHAPTER 12
Austin 3:16

Now, if you're a Steve Austin fan, you know what Austin 3:16 means. If you're not familiar with the term, go ask someone who is. Either way, I can't get specific about Steve's catchphrase here.

Needless to say, after that fateful King of the Ring match, WWF fans were taking notice of Stone Cold Steve Austin. They weren't chanting his name loud enough to raise the rafters off sporting arenas yet, but Steve's time was approaching.

After King of the Ring, signs held by fans bearing the words and numbers "Austin 3:16" could be spotted in house show arenas and on WWF television programming. Fans were starting to appreciate Austin's no-nonsense, take-no-prisoners attitude. Here was a man full of rage who had no respect whatsoever for authority. What many fans didn't realize was that Steve merely had to replay his days in the WCW to give Stone Cold that attitude.

The man who was once told that a wrestler with no gimmick, wearing plain black wrestling tights would never go over with the fans was watching as a group of loyal of fans began to grow.

Steve Austin had served notice to every other wrestler in the WWF by uttering that phrase. Now there was already trouble brewing over Austin's new persona. He was vulgar. He used foul language. He made offensive hand gestures in the ring.

But, as Austin himself has said, parents shouldn't let their impressionable children watch such things.

The WWF was evolving from the family-oriented fare of the 1980s into more adult programming. In the past, wrestlers and storylines were used to sell merchandise. Because most of the wrestling fans in the mid-1980s were young children, professional wrestling was toned down to appeal to children and their parents. Superheroes such as Hulk Hogan and The Ultimate Warrior spawned merchandise like T-shirts, posters, and baseball caps, all aimed at children. But with the growing popularity of the WCW, Vince McMahon decided to steer the WWF in a more sensational direction. Successful TV shock shows, such as *The Jerry Springer Show,* must have been an influence on McMahon's decision. As a result, the WWF became a more violent and adult-oriented program.

Though Vince was not entirely sold on Steve's Stone Cold personality, he let Steve play the character out and put fewer and fewer restrictions on him as time went by.

It was a flexibility that would make Steve the greatest sports entertainment star of the 1990s!

THE BOTTOM LINE: Steve has appeared numerous times as a sports announcer on the MTV clay animation show *Celebrity Death Match.* Once he even fought Vince McMahon on the show (or rather, two pieces of animated clay that looked like Austin and McMahon fought!).

CHAPTER 13
Aiming at The Hitman

Bret "The Hitman" Hart was a wrestler that was the complete opposite of Stone Cold Steve Austin. The Calgary-born Canadian had an impressive and historic run in the WWF. At various times, Bret had been the King of the Ring champion, tag team champion (with Hart Foundation partner Jim Neidhart), Intercontinental Champion (IC; the WWF's version of the U.S. Champion), and WWF World Champion. He was one of the biggest WWF babyfaces when Steve Austin emerged as Stone Cold in the WWF ranks.

Shortly after King of the Ring, Steve began to cut promos about Hart that were insulting and perhaps intended to provoke a feud. Hart, who had taken some time off from the rigors of the WWF, returned to the ring to find a very angry, bald brawler proclaiming "Austin 3:16" in his face.

A rivalry was born between the two very different superstars. Bret still played by the rules, and didn't like the influence he felt Austin was having on WWF fans (especially children). Austin didn't have one ounce of respect for Bret's accomplishments, and wanted to show the world that no one was safe from "Austin 3:16."

Their bitter feud would go down as one of the greatest in WWF history. Bret Hart — the technical, thinking man's wrestler — faced a brawler who had been held back for years, and who had something to prove.

To date, Stone Cold had laid many opponents to waste in the ring, and Bret Hart was the perfect former champion to rise up and meet the challenge of the Texas Rattlesnake. Hart was perceived as a family man, who would often hand out a pair of specially made sunglasses to young fans at ringside. He had defeated many superstars in his WWF run, and was considered (and still is) one of the greatest champions ever to grace the WWF.

Bret was the hero. The man in the white hat. The

babyface who was tired of Stone Cold's venom. The two were heading for a big showdown: The "I Quit" match at Wrestlemania 1997.

THE BOTTOM LINE: Bret Hart has voiced his admiration for Steve Austin, despite the heated rivalry the two shared in the WWF ring.

Vince McMahon, Jr., by and large, is considered the most influential man in professional wrestling. The owner of the WWF is responsible for transforming wrestling from a regional competition, where every state had its own small federation, to bringing the sport into the national spotlight. Vince took the sport out of high school gymnasiums and filled huge arenas across the country and the world.

The WWF is enjoyed by countless fans. The most spectacular wrestling event, which is broadcast annually, is Wrestlemania. Wrestlemania is considered the Superbowl of professional wrestling. It is an event that every wrestling storyline that year leads up to.

For the 1997 Wrestlemania, Stone Cold Steve

Austin and Bret "The Hitman" Hart met in an "I Quit" match. In an "I Quit" match, two combatants battle until one gives up.

Known as a technical wrestling wizard with countless moves in his arsenal (including a deadly submission move, called the Sharpshooter), the odds were definitely in Bret Hart's favor. While it wasn't exactly the main event, it was definitely the second-most anticipated match of the Wrestlemania card.

It was a golden moment for Steve. Only a year before, he had faced an indifferent WWF audience as The Ringmaster. Now here he was, in the biggest show of the year. He was in the second-most important match of the evening. And he was facing Bret "The Hitman" Hart, a WWF legend.

The battle was long, brutal, and bloody. Special guest referee Ken Shamrock, who is considered a fairly tough guy himself, could barely keep order in the ring. Steve opened a gash in his forehead and bled so badly that he could barely see. Austin refused to back down. He fought Hart with everything he had.

The match finally ended when Steve passed out from the blood loss (this, of course, is how it was probably scripted).

Bret Hart was declared the winner, but a valid point was brought up by the ring announcers: Steve Austin had not quit.

To everyone's surprise, the audience began to chant Austin's name. In their eyes, maybe Steve Austin wasn't a babyface good guy or a role model or even a very nice person. But the fans had never seen a wrestler fight so hard to win a match. They respected his efforts and rewarded him with their applause and approval.

Whether it was calculated to happen that way or not, whether Vince McMahon had wanted it or not, it was fairly obvious that . . .

Stone Cold Steve Austin had gone over. . . .

As soon as the match ended, Bret Hart decided to punish Austin some more after the bell had rung. The audience in turn began to boo Hart!

Something incredible had occurred. Austin and Hart had somehow switched roles during the course of the match. At the end of the match, Hart was regarded as the heel, and Stone Cold was regarded as the babyface.

In the weeks following this match, Hart and Austin would continue to collide. Hart scolded the fans for making Austin a hero, and eventually left the WWF for a huge monetary offer from the WCW.

The rivalry between these two wrestlers created some the most unique matches in the WWF and helped cement Steve Austin's place in wrestling history. It's a shame the feud was never resolved before Hart left the WWF.

THE BOTTOM LINE: Steve Austin appeared on *Live with Regis and Kathy Lee* and actually wrestled Regis Philbin!

CHAPTER 15
Cause Stone Cold Said So

After Wrestlemania 13 in 1997, Austin's popularity soared. Soon, packed arenas waited eagerly for the sound of breaking glass . . . the first part of Austin's entrance theme.

Austin would then swagger to the ring while countless Austin 3:16 signs waved. He would enter the square ring, take the microphone, and begin to badger whichever opponent he was gunning for at the moment, ending his tirade with, "And that's the bottom line . . . cause Stone Cold said so!"

On August 3, 1997, at Summerslam, another popular pay-per-view event, Austin faced another Hart. . . . This time, though, it wasn't Bret. It was Owen Hart, Bret's younger brother, who had also built a respectable career in the WWF. (Tragically, Owen later died in 1999 due to a freak wrestling accident.) Owen, the IC champion, was set to defend his title against Stone Cold.

It was a great match. Owen, known for his high-flying moves and technical expertise that nearly rivaled his brother, took Austin to the limit. Toward the climax of the match, Owen hoisted Steve into position for a pile driver, a move in which a wrestler will pick up another wrestler, hold that opponent upside down at the waist, and then drop him on his head. The move is actually an illusion. Usually the wrestler performing the move will cushion his opponent's head with his own knees, ensuring that the opponent will not be harmed.

But that night something went wrong. A slow motion review of the videotape will show that Steve Austin's head was not cushioned when Owen performed the move.

Steve took the full brunt of the move squarely on his head!

After the move had been executed, Owen and the referee anxiously stood by as Steve lay on the mat. He was suffering from a stinger, which is when a wrestler takes a serious blow to the head or neck

Don't mess with Texas! Stone Cold™ Steve Austin tells it like it is.

Austin faces off with the ninth wonder
of the world, Chyna™!

Stone Cold™ turns the tables on his greatest rival, Bret "Hitman™" Hart, by using Hart's move, "the Sharpshooter," against him.

Stone Cold™ sends Marc Mero flying between the ropes.

Stunning Steve Austin, the WWF™ Champion!

Stone Cold™ Steve Austin in a rare
moment outside the ring.

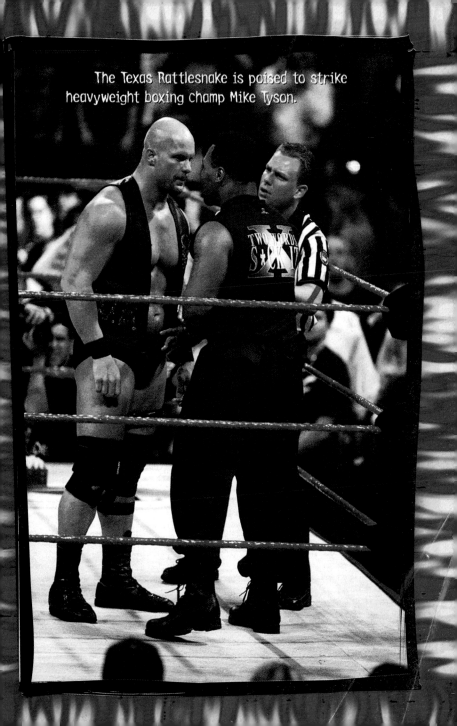

The Texas Rattlesnake is poised to strike heavyweight boxing champ Mike Tyson.

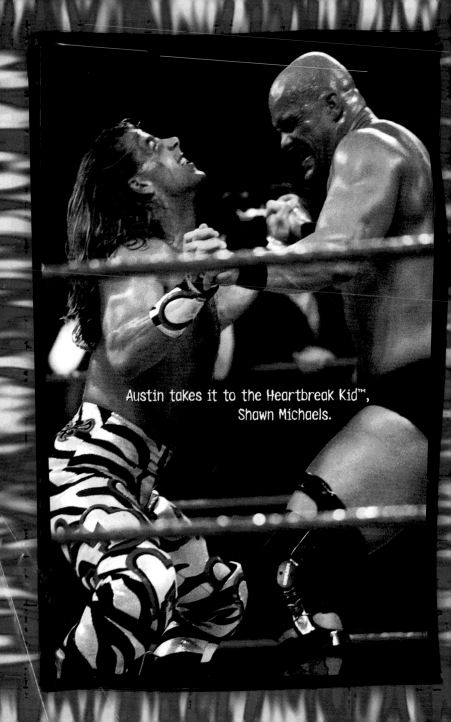

Austin takes it to the Heartbreak Kid™,
Shawn Michaels.

area, and his arms and legs feel numb. It took several seconds for Steve to decide if he could even move.

When he established that he was okay, Steve grabbed Owen's wrestling trunks from behind, pulled him backward, and rolled the surprised Hart brother up for the win.

Steve had to be helped back to the dressing room. Doctors examined him, and informed him that he had spinal trauma. He was ordered to stay out of the wrestling ring.

It was a major drawback for Stone Cold. Months before winning the IC title, Austin and Dude Love (Mick Foley) had won the WWF tag team belts in a Tag Team Championship tournament. He had two pieces of gold around his waist, and a roomful of doctors telling him he might never wrestle again.

Austin was stripped of both titles, and began the process of recovering from his injury. It couldn't have happened at a worse time for him. His popularity was just beginning to soar. Now Stone Cold was grounded — at least, for the moment. But the bottom line was, he was destined to return to the square ring. . . .

THE BOTTOM LINE: During Steve Austin's entrance video, one sequence shows sand running through Steve's hand. Austin has stated that the sand running through his hand symbolizes the time it took for him to become a major superstar!

CHAPTER 16
The Bottom Line

Imagine that you've worked hard for eight years to accomplish a dream. You've wrestled in high schools, eaten nothing but potatoes for days on end, and suffered the humiliation of being fired over the phone by one of your bosses.

As Austin recuperated in his Texas home, these thoughts plagued him. He had worked so hard and so long for the fame he was now enjoying. And he didn't want to lose that popularity before he could return to action.

The doctors may have told Steve he should never wrestle again, but that most certainly went in one ear and out the other. Austin reemerged on WWF programming. In this new storyline, Austin was desperately trying to get back into ring action, but was held back by Vince McMahon because of his medical condition. These were the seeds for the infamous McMahon/Austin feud that would eventually erupt full force.

Austin hunted and stalked McMahon over his ring return. He even used the Stone Cold Stunner on McMahon. McMahon finally agreed to let Austin compete, on one condition: Austin had to sign a waiver that didn't hold the WWF responsible if Austin were hurt in the ring again.

Austin agreed, and returned to action on October 25, 1997. He immediately pulled out his list of WWF superstars, and proceeded to pick up where he left off.

He went through Triple H in a brief feud. At the 1997 Survivor Series pay-per-view, he regained the IC title from Owen Hart. After successfully defending it from up-and-coming star Rocky Maivia at the December 1997 Degeneration X pay-per-view, Austin was ordered to defend it again the following night, on *Monday Night Raw.*

At that point, Rocky Maivia was still molding himself into the electrifying athlete people would one day simply call The Rock™.

Vince McMahon liked the potential of The Rock, and wanted to see him get another IC title shot against Austin, but Stone Cold refused to defend the title that night. Instead, he found a bridge across a river and tossed the belt into the water below. Rocky was awarded the championship, but that was fine with Steve. He had bigger goals.

It was time for the Texas Rattlesnake to zero in on the WWF world title.

THE BOTTOM LINE: Steve Austin and Brian Pillman feuded briefly in the WWF in 1997, until Brian's tragic death.

CHAPTER 17
The Marked Man

The Royal Rumble is a pay-per-view event in which 30 wrestlers enter the ring one at a time and eliminate foes by tossing them over the top rope. This continues until one man is left. The winner gets a title shot at Wrestlemania.

Weeks before the January 18, 1998, airing of the Royal Rumble, Steve Austin attacked about a dozen other wrestlers, using his Stunner on them. The wrestlers he attacked were fellow participants of the upcoming Royal Rumble.

Stone Cold was serving notice. He publicly vowed to win the Royal Rumble and face the WWF champion at Wrestlemania 14.

The night of January 18, 1998, Austin kept his vow. Opponent after opponent fell to the Texas

Rattlesnake's wrath. He emerged as the winner of the Royal Rumble. Austin would get his world title shot at the main event at Wrestlemania. In attendance at the Royal Rumble was boxing heavyweight Mike Tyson, who cheered for Austin from the audience.

During the next WWF *Monday Night Raw,* Vince McMahon made a major announcement about Wrestlemania. Wrestlemania is famous for its celebrity guests. Vince brought out Mike Tyson and announced that Tyson would be the special guest enforcer referee for the Wrestlemania main event.

McMahon nearly fainted when Steve Austin's music exploded into the arena. Austin stepped into the ring and had a face-off with Tyson. The two got into a shoving match, and had to be separated by security.

Of course, this was an act. But it was still impressive seeing Austin stand up to a ferocious boxer like Mike Tyson. The next day, headlines and news programs across the country ran the story.

Stone Cold Steve Austin would face The Heartbreak Kid, Shawn Michaels, at Wrestlemania 14, with Mike Tyson as the guest referee enforcer.

At this time, Shawn Michaels had started his own stable, Degeneration X. Along with Triple H and

Chyna, their female bodyguard, he waged a war against the establishment of Vince McMahon.

During a television segment, Shawn confronted Mike Tyson. The two exchanged words, then Shawn ripped Mike's shirt off, revealing a Degeneration X T-shirt underneath! The shouting match had been a trick all along! Mike Tyson was on Degeneration X's side!

What chance did Austin have of winning the WWF world title now?

THE BOTTOM LINE: Stone Cold loves country music, but has also said he enjoys rap music, too!

CHAPTER 18
A Stone Cold Champion

Now, before we go into the Wrestlemania 14 match that pitted Steve Austin against Shawn Michaels with Mike Tyson as special guest referee enforcer, let's make sure we're clear on something else.

As most of you probably know, professional wrestling is a scripted affair. It's not exactly fake, because of the athleticism and risk of injury that are involved. But wrestling is similar to an action movie. It's a form of entertainment with trained stuntmen executing flawless moves.

So, when you read about the following match, understand that it was scripted and predetermined before anybody entered the ring.

Austin and Michaels went at it during the main

event of Wrestlemania 14. While Austin is known as a brawler who can stomp a mud hole into an opponent and walk it dry, Shawn Michaels is no slouch himself. He has been regarded as the most resilient WWF champion of all time. He had defeated men stronger than him. Men larger than him. He was referred to on many occasions as "The Giant Killer." His Superkick, a kick to his opponent's chin (appropriately dubbed "Sweet Chin Music"), was a finisher that had ended many of Michaels's matches.

Michaels, a Texas native himself, was a perfect match for Austin. Michaels had long blond hair, was flashy, and coined himself "The Heartbreak Kid" because of his good looks.

A younger Stunning Steve Austin shared many similarities with Michaels. But the no-nonsense Stone Cold Steve Austin was out to prove that spandex and a pretty face could not withstand the burning anger that was building up inside of him.

It was Austin's time. For eight years, destiny had been an elusive prize. But now Steve could feel it. Feel it from the Wrestlemania crowd that chanted his name.

The match was spectacular. Michaels used his

high-flying aerial moves and had Steve on the ropes many times. Austin countered with fists and boots, beating Michaels down into a corner post whenever he could ground the champion.

Austin finally executed his deadly finisher, the Stunner, on Michaels. He covered the fallen champion closely for the three count. Mike Tyson made the count, and then decked the argumentative Michaels, who started a shoving match with the boxing great. Tyson had a change of heart and even raised Stone Cold's arm in victory.

The Texas Rattlesnake had made it to the top of the wrestling game. He had proved all of his critics of the past wrong.

Stone Cold Steve Austin was the WWF World Champion.

With the interest and controversy surrounding Stone Cold Steve Austin, the WWF began to regain its popularity and started to beat the rival WCW in the ratings war.

Steve Austin lost and regained the WWF world title four times in brutal feuds with The Undertaker, Kane, Mankind, and The Rock.

But there was one rival who would stand out from all of the opponents Steve Austin had ever faced.

One opponent who would plague Steve for a very long time: WWF owner Vince McMahon.

THE BOTTOM LINE: Steve Austin appeared in a very funny 1-800-COLLECT commercial with fellow WWF grappler, D'Lo Brown.

CHAPTER 19
Stone Cold Versus Vince McMahon

To understand the chain of events that led to the famous Stone Cold Steve Austin and Vince McMahon feud, you have to consider a couple of things.

Again — yes again — let's drag that speck of reality into the wrestling storyline. Steve Austin had been treated badly by the powers that be in the WCW. He was held back even when his popularity began to increase. He was fired over the phone. To say Steve Austin had a problem with authority would be an understatement. Steve had fought authority his whole career. When told he was lacking charisma and a gimmick, he worked hard and tried to show everybody — audiences and wrestling management alike — that he had what it took to set the square ring on fire.

Deep down, he had known better all along. It had just taken him a while to find the character of Stone Cold Steve Austin . . . the brooding, dissatisfied Texas Rattlesnake that had been building deep down inside of him for years. The character was fueled by the anger and frustration Steve had felt because of his treatment by other wrestling federations.

Vince McMahon capitalized on this by fabricating a unique storyline. Stone Cold Steve Austin, the gruff, vulgar Texan now held the WWF championship. As the owner of the WWF, Vince McMahon could not tolerate having a champion like Stone Cold Steve Austin. WWF champions of yesteryear were heroic figures, who would hold babies for photographs and teach kids to walk the straight and narrow. Stone Cold Steve Austin taught his fans to question authority and give it the Stone Cold Stunner. He told his audience to trust nobody. His vulgar hand gestures and choice of drink in the ring were causing commotion from parents who thought the WWF was becoming a bad influence on their children.

Vince tried to take Steve aside and mold him into an appropriate WWF champion. But Steve would have none of it. "Uh-uh!" When this approach didn't work, Vince set out to make Austin's career a living nightmare. He did everything in his corporate power to dethrone the Texas Rattlesnake. While Vince succeeded in his quest to take his precious WWF world title from Austin, Steve would come right back for more, and find a way to "stunner" himself back to the championship.

Surely, Steve worked out a lot of frustration by playing out this storyline with Vince. And Vince succeeded in creating the biggest heel in the WWF: himself.

Stone Cold Steve Austin was on top of the wrestling world. His merchandise, like the Austin 3:16 T-shirt, topped the list in sales. His reign of terror continued for close to two years, and there seemed to be no sign of it stopping. But then, all good things must come to an end . . .

THE BOTTOM LINE: Steve had a personalized WWF world championship belt created. It features the image of a smoking skull.

CHAPTER 20
And That's All I Got to Say About That!

In late 1999, Steve complained of pain and numbness in his legs, arms, and hands. He was diagnosed with a bone spur touching his spinal cord. Steve underwent major back surgery, and has been recovering from the injury ever since.

The WWF has pushed other wrestlers in Steve's long absence. Wrestlers like The Rock, Triple H, and Chris Jericho are currently enjoying stardom in the WWF.

However, there is a noticeable gap in the federation. Many of the current WWF superstars now exhibit traits similar to Steve Austin's, perhaps trying to recreate the mixture that ignited his career.

But there is only one Stone Cold Steve Austin.

And it is his adamant belief that he will one day return to the wrestling ring.

While fans wait for his health to allow this return, they can console themselves with the fact that Austin has found a secondary career: acting.

Austin has appeared numerous times on the CBS cop show *Nash Bridges*. Playing the motorcycle-riding, tough-as-nails cop, Jake Cage, Austin helped the show receive its highest ratings to date. There has even been talk of creating a Jake Cage show for CBS.

Austin has also appeared on the *Live With Regis and Kathie Lee* Show, MTV's *Celebrity Deathmatch,* and a 1-800-COLLECT commercial.

Even with the option of pursuing a career in acting, however, Austin longs to return to the ring and restart a legacy of chaos that feels incomplete.

Even if he is never able to physically compete in the square ring again, Steve shouldn't worry. He has left his mark on the history of sports entertainment. He could always work in some other capacity for the WWF. He could scout talent, and be a mentor to up-and-coming wrestlers who feel the torment he once felt. Perhaps he could even become a match commentator.

But one thing is for certain: Stone Cold Steve Austin will return to the public eye in some manner, coiled and ready to strike out at us like the Texas Rattlesnake he is.

And that's the bottom line . . .

THE BOTTOM LINE: Steve is currently engaged to Debra McMichael, a WWF personality who has managed WWF wrestlers.

The Steve Austin Wrestling Time Line

- Late 1989 — Beat Frogman LaBlanc in his first match at the Sportatorium in Dallas, Texas.
- 1990 — Had a feud with Chris Adams in the USWA that earned him the *Pro Wrestling Illustrated* Rookie of the Year Award.
- May 31, 1991 — Debuted in WCW.
- June 3, 1991 — Defeated Bobby Eaton for the WCW Television Title.
- March 2, 1993 — With tag team partner Brian Pillman, defeated Ricky Steamboat and Shane Douglas for the WCW tag team titles.
- 1993 — Defeated Dusty Rhodes to become the WCW U.S. Champion.
- Fall 1995 — Debuted in the ECW.
- December 18, 1995 — Debuted as The Ringmas-

ter in the WWF. Had an unbeaten streak until February, 1996.

- June 23, 1996 — Now known as Stone Cold Steve Austin, won the 1996 King of the Ring Tournament.
- 1997 — Began famous feud with Bret "The Hitman" Hart.
- May 26, 1997 — With Shawn Michaels, defeated Owen Hart and Davey Boy Smith for the WWF tag team titles.
- 1997 included fall dates like September 7, 1999 Summerslam — Defeated Owen Hart to become the WWF Intercontinental Champion.
- October 25, 1997 — Returned to in-ring action.
- January 18, 1998 — Won the Royal Rumble.
- 1998 March Wrestlemania 14 — Defeated Shawn Michaels to become WWF World Champion.
- June 28, 1998 — Lost world title to Kane.
- June 29, 1998 — Regained world title from Kane.
- July 26, 1998 — With The Undertaker, defeated Dude Love and Kane for the WWF tag team belts.
- September 27, 1998 — Lost world title in a three-way match against The Undertaker and Kane.
- January, 1999 — Won the Royal Rumble.
- March 28, 1999 Wrestlemania 15 — Defeated The Rock to become WWF World Champion.

- May 23, 1999 — Lost world title to The Undertaker.
- September 7, 1999 — Ordered to give up his tag
  team and IC titles due to injury and inability to
  defend them.

Stone Cold University

Take to the following test to see how well you know the Texas Rattlesnake. Answer more than 20 correctly, and you could earn a degree from Stone Cold University!

1. Where did Steve Austin go to high school?
   a.   Edna High School
   b.   Victoria High School
   c.   Austin High School
2. Who ran the school where Austin trained to become a wrestler?
   a.   Vince McMahon
   b.   Eric Bischoff
   c.   Chris Adams

3. Who was Steve's Hollywood Blonds tag team partner in the WCW?

    a.   Steven Regal

    b.   Brian Pillman

    c.   Dusty Rhodes

4. Who was the WCW executive who fired Steve Austin?

    a.   Eric Bischoff

    b.   Ric Flair

    c.   Jim Duggan

5. What was Steve's wrestling name in the WCW?

    a.   Sensational Steve Austin

    b.   Stunning Steve Austin

    c.   The Bionic Man, Steve Austin

6. What is Steve Austin's real name?

    a.   Steve Williams

    b.   Don Hughes

    c.   Peter Simmons

7. What is the name of Stone Cold's finishing maneuver?

    a.   The Rattlesnake Strike

    b.   Don't Trust Anybody

    c.   The Stone Cold Stunner

8. What is Austin 3:16?

a. Stone Cold's catchphrase

b. The time of day Steve was born

c. The time of day Steve works out

9. Who was the first WWF wrestler that Austin had a major feud with?

a. The Undertaker

b. Bret Hart

c. Doink, the clown

10. Why did Vince McMahon become Steve Austin's number-one enemy?

a. Steve took the last doughnut backstage

b. Vince didn't feel Steve was championship material

c. Steve accidentally dented Vince's limousine.

11. Which boxer was named a guest referee enforcer for Steve's Wrestlemania 14 match against Shawn Michaels?

a. Muhammad Ali

b. Joe Frasier

c. Mike Tyson

12. Which one of these shows has Steve Austin NOT appeared on?

a. *Celebrity Death Match*

b. *Nash Bridges*

c.   *Buffy the Vampire Slayer*

13. Which WCW wrestler looks very similar to
    Steve Austin?
        a.   Buff Bagwell
        b.   Goldberg
        c.   Vampiro

14. Who did Steve dress up like and imperson-
    ate while in the WCW?
        a.   Marc Mero
        b.   Doink, the clown
        c.   Hulk Hogan

15. In what year did Steve have his first
    wrestling match?
        a.   1986
        b.   1987
        c.   1989

16. Who did Steve defeat at the 1996 King of
    the Ring to become the winner?
        a.   Jake Roberts
        b.   Triple H
        c.   Vince McMahon

17. Who did Steve defeat the first time he be-
    came WWF champion?
        a.   Bret Hart
        b.   The Undertaker
        c.   Shawn Michaels

18. Which one is NOT a Stone Cold catch-
    phrase?
    a.   "Cause Stone Cold Said So."
    b.   "Don't Trust Anybody."
    c.   "Why Can't We Be Friends?"
19. Before becoming a wrestler, Steve worked
    as a:
    a.   Hollywood actor
    b.   Dockworker
    c.   Dressmaker
20. When he was first introduced to the WWF
    fans, Steve was known as:
    a.   The Ringmaster
    b.   The Texas Rattlesnake
    c.   The Tough Guy
21. Who was Steve's manager when he first
    entered the WWF?
    a.   Shane McMahon
    b.   Paul Bearer
    c.   Ted DiBiase
22. Steve has a tattoo on his calf. What is it?
    a.   The State of Texas
    b.   A smoking skull
    c.   Austin 3:16
23. Before entering the WWF, Steve worked
    briefly for what smaller federation?

a. The Texas Wrestling Alliance
b. The East Coast Wrestling Organization
c. Extreme Championship Wrestling

24. While wrestling in Japan, which muscle did Steve injure?
    a. Tricep
    b. Calf
    c. Pectoral

25. Who did Steve defeat to win the WCW United States Championship?
    a. Rick Rude
    b. Brian Pillman
    c. Dusty Rhodes

Answers: 1-a; 2-c; 3-b; 4-a; 5-b; 6-a; 7-c; 8-a; 9-b; 10-b; 11-c; 12-c; 13-b; 14-c; 15-c; 16-a; 17-c; 18-c; 19-b; 20-a; 21-c; 22-a; 23-c; 24-a; 25-c

If you answered 20–25 questions correctly: Congratulations! You have earned a degree from the Stone Cold University!

10–19: Good show, but you still have a lot to learn about the Texas Rattlesnake!

0–9: You better flip back and review this book again!

Wrestling Terms

Anklelock — A painful submission move in which a wrestler twists an opponent's ankle until the opponent submits. Made famous by wrestler Ken Shamrock.

Babyface — Term used for a good guy wrestler.

Backflip — A wrestler picks up an opponent and tosses him backward, over his head.

Bodyslam — The most common move. A wrestler picks up an opponent and slams him to the mat.

Bodysplash — When a high-flying wrestler has an opponent down, he may finish the match with this move. The high flyer climbs to the top turnbuckle, then leaps onto his opponent, bringing down his body weight on the fallen foe. Made popular by Jimmy Snuka.

Bumps — When a wrestler is flipped, thrown, or falls to the mat, he is trained to take bumps, so he doesn't get seriously hurt.

Cage match — A match that takes place inside a steel cage with four walls but no ceiling. The winner is the first wrestler who can climb out of the cage.

Card — The line-up of matches in a wrestling event.

Clothesline — A wrestler charges his opponent and knocks him down with an outstretched arm.

Coffin match — Made famous by The Undertaker. The wrestler who manages to put his opponent in a coffin and close the lid wins the match.

Double-armed DDT — A move that is performed by grabbing the opponent mid-waist and dropping him on his head.

Dropkick — A wrestler jumps into the air and kicks an opponent.

Dumpster match — A free-for-all match in which the winning wrestler must put his opponent in a metal dumpster and close the lid. Any items found in the dumpster can be used to attack an opponent.

Finishing move — A move perfected by a wrestler that will finish a match. For instance, Mankind's finishing move is the Mandible Claw. When he uses this move, the match is over.

Gimmick — Something a wrestler does, wears, or says to make their wrestling character work with an audience. For instance, a wrestler claiming to be a fireman might wear a fireman's suit to the ring.

Going over — Term used to describe a wrestler becoming popular with fans.

Heat — Heat is boos from fans. Heels get heat from an audience.

Heel — Term used for a bad guy wrestler.

High flyer — A wrestler who uses many aerial moves in his performance.

Jobber — A wrestler just starting out, who is instructed to lose to the more experienced talent of a federation.

Kick out — A wrestler kicks out of a pin attempt before the referee counts to three.

Leg drop — A move made famous by Hulk Hogan. While the opponent is lying on the mat, the wrestler drops a leg on the opponent's head.

Mid-carder — A wrestler that is not considered a jobber, but still hasn't made the main event of a card.

Million dollar dream — A name for the finishing move Steve Austin used as The Ringmaster. Same move as a sleeper hold.

Pedigree — Finishing move in which a wrestler puts his opponent's head between his legs, hooks both of his arms, drops to his knees, and sends the opponent's face crashing to the mat with his weight behind it. Used by Triple H.

Pile driver — Considered one of the deadliest wrestling moves. A wrestler holds the opponent upside down and drops him on his head.

Pinned — A wrestler is pinned when his opponent manages to pin his shoulders to the mat for a three-count made by a referee.

Samoan drop (or backdrop) — A wrestler picks up his opponent, holds the opponent on his shoulders, and then falls backward. The opponent hits the mat, taking the brunt of the move. Made famous by The Rock, but used by many Samoan wrestlers.

Sharpshooter — A submission hold that is a version of the classic Boston crab. The wrestler twists the opponent's legs and flips him onto his stomach. He then sits on the opponent's back while applying pressure to the legs. This move strains the opponent's knees and lower back. It was made famous by Bret Hart.

Shoot interview — When a wrestler is allowed to improvise during an interview segment.

Sleeper hold — A move that cuts off oxygen to a wrestler's brain, causing him to pass out.

Stone Cold Stunner — Steve Austin's finishing move. Used when Steve turns his back to his opponent, grabs his opponent's head and positions it on his shoulder, and drops to his knees, driving his opponent's weight down onto his chin.

Submission hold — A hold designed to cause the wrestler so much pain that he gives up the match. When the wrestler taps the mat, the referee rings the bell, and the other wrestlers wins.

Suplex — A wrestler raises his opponent in the air and drops him flat on his back.

Tag team match — A match in which two wrestlers battle two other wrestlers. One man from each team starts the match, then has to tag his partner, who, until he is tagged, remains on the outside of the ring.

Three-way — This match boasts three men fighting at once. The first man to score a pin wins. However, when three wrestlers are fighting at once, it is very difficult for a pin to be scored.

Title holder — A wrestler with a championship belt.

Turnbuckle — A turnbuckle is found in every corner of the ring. It holds up the ring ropes . . . but many wrestlers ram their opponent's head into the padded steel!